THE CRUCIBLE IN HISTORY
AND OTHER ESSAYS

ARTHUR MILLER

THE CRUCIBLE
IN HISTORY
AND OTHER ESSAYS

Methuen

Published by Methuen 2005

1 3 5 7 9 10 8 6 4 2

First published in hardback in 2000 by Methuen Publishing Ltd
11–12 Buckingham Gate, London, SW1E 6LB

The Crucible in History & Behind *The Price*
Copyright © Arthur Miller 2000
Salesman at Fifty © Arthur Miller 1998

The right of Arthur Miller to be identified as the author
of this book has been asserted by him in accordance with the
Copyright, Designs and Patents Act 1988.

A CIP catalogue record for this book is available from the British Library

ISBN 0 413 77524 0

Typeset by Deltatype Ltd, Birkenhead, Merseyside
Printed and bound in Great Britain by
Bookmarque Ltd, Croydon, Surrey

Contents

The Crucible in History

The Crucible In History

The Massey Lecture, Harvard University

It would probably never have occurred to me to write a play about the Salem witch trials of 1692 had I not seen some astonishing correspondences with that calamity in the America of the late forties and early fifties. There were other enticements for me in the Salem period, however, most especially the chance it offered to write in what was for me a practically new language, one that would require new muscles.

I was never a scholar or an historian, of course; my basic need was somehow to respond to a phenomenon which, with only small exaggeration, one could say was paralysing a whole generation and in an amazingly short time was drying up the habits of trust and toleration in public discourse. I refer, of course, to the anti-communist rage, that threatened to reach hysterical proportions and sometimes did. I can't remember anyone calling it an ideological war but I think now that that is what it amounted to. Looking back at the period, I suppose we very rapidly passed over anything like a discussion or debate, and into something quite different, a hunt not just for subversive people but for ideas and even a suspect language. The object, a shock at the time, was to destroy the least credibility of any and all ideas associated with socialism and communism, whose proponents were assumed to be either knowing or unwitting agents of Soviet subversion. An ideological war is like guerrilla war, since the enemy is first of all an idea whose proponents are not in uniform but are disguised as ordinary citizens, a situation that can scare a lot of people to death.

I am not really equipped to deliver a history of Cold War America, which, like any other period, is packed with passionately held illusions and ideas distorted on all sides by fear. Suffice to say it was a time of great, no doubt unprecedented fear; but fear, like love, is mostly incommunicable once it has passed. So I shall try to limit myself, as far as possible, to speak of events as they struck me personally, for those are what finally created *The Crucible*.

One knew that Congressional investigations of subversion had been going on since the thirties. The Dies Committee, beginning with Nazi subversion in America, ended up with a never-ending and often silly investigation of communists. But the country in the thirties was not under external threat and nobody seemed to take seriously any menace from an American Communist Party that could hardly elect a dog-catcher. From my perspective, what changed everything was the victory of the Chinese communists in 1949. Inevitably, the Chinese reds were seen as all but an arm of the expansionist post-Second World War Soviet machine, and a look at the map would indeed show that an enormous new part of the planet had turned red.

'Who Lost China!' almost instantly became the Republican mantra. Who were the traitors inside the Democratic administrations going back to Roosevelt that had sold out our favourite Chinese, Chiang Kai-shek? This, I think, was the first notable injection of the idea of treason and foreign agents into domestic political discourse. To me the simplicity of it all was breathtaking. There had to be left-wing traitors in government, otherwise how could the the Chinese – who, as everyone knew, loved Americans more than anybody – have turned against the pro-American Chiang Kai-shek in favour of a Soviet agent like Mao Tse-tung?

All I knew about China in 1949 was what I had read in Edgar Snow and Jack Belden and Teddy White and other American reporters. What it amounted to was that the Nationalist regime was feudal and thoroughly corrupt and that the reds were basically a miserably exploited peasantry which at long last had risen up and thrown their exploiters into the sea. I thought it was a great idea. In any event, the idea of our 'losing' China seemed the equivalent of a flea losing an elephant. Nevertheless there was a growing uproar in and out of Congress. One read that the China Lobby, a wealthy support group backing Chiang Kai-shek's efforts to return to Beijing from Taiwan, was reportedly paying a lot of the bills, and that Senator McCarthy was one of their most effective champions. The partisan political manipulation of a real issue was so patent that President Truman could dismiss the Republican scare as a 'red herring'. But it is an indication of its impact on the public mind that he soon had to retreat and institute a Loyalty Board of his own to investigate the allegiance of government employees.

The Chinese Revolution was always central to the fear of the reds and remained so to the end of McCarthy's magical sway over the country. For example, when at long last Edward R. Murrow, CBS's chief correspondent, finally decided to take on the Senator, who by then had been weakened by the puncturing of his own overblown exaggerations, McCarthy was given air-time to respond to Murrow's barbs, and facing the camera simply displayed a wall-sized map of Russia, and then expanded it until it showed China alongside, saying in effect, here is Russia, and now they have the teeming land-mass of China added on. Then, with his usual hambone, through-the-nose foreboding, he turned straight into the camera and announced, 'Edward R. Murrow is a card-carrying member of the American Civil Liberties Union!' It no longer worked – most star-turns have a certain limited shelf-life; but even at the time it was striking how the Chinese reds were so incendiary to the prevalent fearfulness.

To call the ensuing atmosphere paranoid is not to

say that there was nothing real in the American–Soviet stand-off. To be sure I am far more willing than I was then, owing to some experiences of my own with both sides, to credit both American and Soviet leaderships with enough ignorance of each other to have ignited a third world war. But if there was one element that lent the conflict a tone of the inauthentic, the spurious and the invented it was the swiftness with which all values were being forced in a matter of months literally to reverse themselves. I recall some examples.

Death of a Salesman opened in February of 1949 and was hailed by nearly every newspaper and magazine. Parenthetically, I should add that two exceptions come to mind, one Marxist the other ex-Marxist: the Marxist being the *Daily Worker*, which found the play defeatist and lacking militant protest; and the ex-Marxist Mary McCarthy, who seemed outraged by the idea of elevating it to the status of tragedy and just hated it in general, particularly, I thought, because it was so popular. As all participants in the higher dispensation understood, the mark of real tragedy was that it always closed in two weeks. Anyway, several movie studios wanted it and it was finally Columbia Pictures that bought it, and engaged a great star, Frederick March, to play Willy.

In something like two years or less, as I recall, with the picture finished, I was asked by a terrified Columbia to sign an anti-communist declaration in order to ward off picket lines, which the American Legion was threatening to throw across the entrances of theatres showing the film. In the numerous phone calls that followed, the air of panic was heavy. It was the first intimation of what would soon follow. I declined to make any such statement which frankly I found demeaning; what right had any organization to demand anyone's pledge of loyalty? I was sure the whole thing would soon go away, it was just too outrageous.

But instead of the problem disappearing, the studio, it now developed, had actually made another film, a short which was to be shown with *Salesman*. This was called *The Life of a Salesman* and consisted of several lectures by City College School of Business professors. What they boiled down to was that selling was basically a joy, one of the most gratifying and useful of professions, and that Willy was simply a nut. Never in show-business history has a studio spent so much good money to prove that its feature film was pointless. I threatened to sue (on what basis I had no idea) but of course the short could not be shown lest it bore the audience blind. But in less than two years *Death of a Salesman* had gone from being a master-piece to being a heresy, and a fraudulent one at that.

In 1948, '49, '50, '51, I had the sensation of being trapped inside a perverse work of art, one of those Escher constructs in which it is impossible to make out whether a stairway is going up or down. Practically everyone I knew, all survivors of the Great Depression of course, as well as the Second World War, stood somewhere within the conventions of the political left of centre; one or two were Communist

Party members, some were sort of fellow travellers, as I suppose I was, and most had had one or another brush with Marxist ideas or organizations. I have never been able to believe in the reality of these people being actual or putative traitors any more than I could be, yet others like them were being fired from teaching or jobs in government or large corporations. The surreality of it all never left me. We were living in an art form, a metaphor that had no long history but had suddenly, incredibly enough, gripped the country. In today's terms, the country had been delivered into the hands of the radical Right, a ministry of free-floating apprehension toward absolutely anything that never happens in the middle of Missouri. It is always with us, this anxiety, sometimes directed toward foreigners, Jews, Catholics, fluoridated water, aliens in space, masturbation, homosexuality, or the Internal Revenue Department. But in the fifties any of these could be validated as real threats by rolling out a map of China. And if this seems crazy now it seemed just as crazy then, but openly doubting it could cost you.

So I suppose that in one sense *The Crucible* was an attempt to make life real again, palpable and structured. One hoped that a work of art might illuminate the tragic absurdities of an anterior work of art that was called reality, but was not.

Again, it was the very swiftness of the change that lent it this surreality. Only three or four years earlier an American movie audience, on seeing a newsreel of – let's say – a Russian soldier or even Stalin saluting the Red Army, would have applauded, for that army had taken the brunt of the Nazi onslaught, as most people were aware. Now they would have looked on with fear or at least bewilderment, for the Russians had become the enemy of mankind, a menace to all that was good. It was the Germans who, with amazing rapidity, were turning good. Could this be real? And how, mentally, to deal with, for example, American authorities removing from books in German schools any mention of the Hitler decade?

In the unions, communists and their allies, who had been known as intrepid organizers, were now to be shorn of union membership and turned out as seditious. Harry Bridges, for example, the idol of West Coast longshoremen, whom he had all but single-handedly organized, would be subjected to court trial after court trial to drive him out of the country and back to his native Australia as an unadmitted communist. Academics, some of them prominent in their fields, were especially targeted, many forced to retire or simply fired for disloyalty. Some of them were communists, some were fellow travellers and, inevitably, a certain number were simply unaffiliated liberals refusing to sign one of the dozens of humiliating anti-communist pledges being required by terrified college administrations.

The sweep went not only very wide but also very deep. By 1950 or thereabouts there were subjects one would do better to avoid, and even words that were best left unspoken. The Spanish Civil War, for example, had quickly become a hot button. That war, as some of you may not recall, resulted from an attack in 1936 by the military upon the democratically elected socialist government. After three years of terrible fighting, in which the Luftwaffe's planes and Mussolini's troops gave him crucial help, the fascist General Franco took power. Spain would become the very symbol of the struggle against fascism; but more and more one heard, after about 1950, that Franco's victory was actually a not unworthy triumph of anti-communists. This, despite the common belief through the forties that, had Franco been thrown-back, opening Hitler's whole Atlantic flank to hostile democrats rather than allied fascists, his war against Europe might well have had to be postponed, if not aborted.

Again, it was the swiftness of this change that made it so fictional to me. Occasionally these sudden turnarounds were rather comical, which didn't help one's sense of reality.

One day in 1950 or thereabouts, a stranger called, asking to come and see me about some matter he preferred not to talk about on the phone, and dropping as one of his bona fides that he had fought in Spain. I figured he was in trouble politically and must be really desperate to imagine I could help him. (A few ill-informed people still imagined I had some clout of this kind.) He arrived at my Brooklyn Heights house, a bright youngish fellow carrying a briefcase. We chatted for a few minutes and then got down to business. From his briefcase he unfolded a desk-sized map of a Texas oilfield, and pointing at various black dots explained that these were oil wells in which he was selling stock. When I confessed surprise that an idealistic anti-fascist fighter should end up as an oil-stock salesman, he asked, 'Why not?' and with a touch of noble sincerity added, 'Once the workers take over they're going to need oil!' This was a harbinger of the wondrous rationalizations that I would have cause to recall as our future arrived. But I really should add that while all this was new to us it was a very old story in many other places where dictatorships had come and gone, where people had long since learned how to laugh internally without creasing a cheek.

My view of things as uneasily 'fictional' turned out not to be entirely unwarranted; some six or seven years later, in one of the more elaborate episodes of my experience, I would be cited for contempt of Congress for refusing to identify writers I had met at one of the two communist writers' meetings I had attended many years before. Normally, these citations resulted in a routine Federal Court trial which wound up in half an hour with an inevitable conviction. But my lawyer, Joseph L. Rauh, Jr, brought in a former senator, Harry M. Cain of Washington, who had been head of the Loyalty Board under Eisenhower, to testify as an expert witness that my plays showed no signs of having been written under communist discipline. Until then, 'expert witnesses' had always been FBI men or ex-communists. Cain had a very different and curious history: a decorated Korean War veteran and fierce anti-communist, he had been a sidekick of McCarthy's and a weekly poker partner. But disillusionment had worn him down when, as head of the Loyalty Board, he had had to deal with an amazing load of letters arriving each morning from people suspecting employers or employees, neighbours, friends, relatives and the corner grocer of communist sympathies. The idea of the whole country spying on itself began to depress him, and looking down from his office window he had the overwhelming idea of a terrified nation out there – and worse, that some substantial fraction of it had become quite literally crazed.

The breaking point for him came with a series of relentlessly persistent letters from a Baltimore postman complaining of having been fired for disloyalty. What bothered him was the handwriting, which was barely literate. Communists were bad people but they were rarely illiterate. Finally, Cain invited the man to his office and soon realized that the accusations were simply not credible; this led him to wonder about the hundreds of other accusations he had been regularly forwarding to the FBI with little or no examination. At last he went directly to Eisenhower and told him he was convinced that the Loyalty Board itself was incompatible with political liberty. The next morning he found himself fired. It seems that handling all that disloyalty had infected him, too.

That was still six or seven years on. My brushes with this fictional world I would soon inhabit went back to 1947, when *All My Sons*, as the result of protests by the Catholic War Veterans, was removed from the US Army's theatrical repertoire in Europe. It was deemed a threat to soldiers' morale, since it told the story of a manufacturer selling defective parts to the Air Force. In a few years an ex-officer in that theatrical troupe wrote to inform me that not only had *All My Sons* been banned, but also an order had come down that no other play written by Arthur Miller was to be produced by the Army. As far as the Army was concerned, I had simply disappeared as an American writer.

But you never know – sometimes a bad experience can turn out to be useful. In the late sixties, as President of International Pen, the London-based, worldwide writers' organization, I would find myself commiserating with Soviet, Chinese, Czech, Hungarian writers, and those in other Communist countries who had seen their names obliterated from the rosters of living authors. Of course the so-called Socialist Bloc was far from alone in this practice; the South African Apartheid regime was probably more ruthless as a censor, not to mention the long list of right-wing, fascistic Latin American regimes. If there was a unique element in the American repression, it was the widespread assumption that it didn't exist. The demonization of the Left had been so thorough as to justify what in effect was its illegalization and then its disappearance, and without the government or many people admitting that it was not simply the zeitgeist that had sort of blown it away.

But it is impossible, certainly in this short time, to convey properly the fears that marked that period.

Nobody was being shot, to be sure, although some were going to jail, where at least one, a man named William Remington, was murdered by an inmate hoping to shorten his sentence for having killed a communist. Rather than physical fear it was the sense of impotence, which seemed to deepen with each passing week, of being unable to speak simply and accurately of the very recent past when being left-wing in America, and for that matter in Europe, was simply to be alive to the dilemmas of the day. To be sure, I had counted myself a radical since my years in college and had tried and failed to read *Das Kapital*; but the Marxist formulations had certainly given shape to my views on politics – fundamentally that to understand a political phenomenon you had to look for the money. (Which is also why businessmen understand Marxism better than anybody.) It also meant that you believed capitalism was quite possibly doomed, but during and after the Great Depression there were times when not to believe that would have put you in a political minority. I may have dreamed of a socialism where people no longer lived off another's labour, but I had never met a spy.

As for the very idea of willingly subjecting my work not only to some party's discipline but to anyone's control, my repugnance was such that, as a very young and indigent writer, I had turned down fairly lucrative offers to work for Hollywood studios because of a helpless revulsion at the thought of someone other than myself literally owning the paper I was typing on. It would not be long, perhaps four or five years, before the fraudulence of Soviet cultural claims was as clear to me as it should have been earlier. But I would never have found it believable, either in the fifties or later, that with its thuggish self-righteousness and callous contempt for artists' freedoms, the unabashed Soviet way of controlling culture could be successfully exported to America. The possible exception, perhaps, might be Madison Avenue advertising agencies where ideological control over artists is taken for granted as a condition of employment. In any case, to believe in that danger generally I would have had to share a bed with the Republican Right.

Which is not to say that there was no sincerity in the fears people felt in the fifties, and – as in most things human – much cynicism as well, if not corruption. The moral high ground, as in most things human, was wreathed in fog. But the stubborn fact remained that some greatly talented people were being driven out of the country to live and work in England, screenwriters like Carl Foreman and Donald Ogden Stewart, actors like Charlie Chaplin and Sam Wanamaker, who, incidentally, in his last years led the campaign to build the replica of Shakespeare's theatre on the Thames. I no longer recall the total number of our political exiles, but it was more than too many and too disgraceful for a nation prideful of its democracy.

Writing now, almost half a century later, with the Soviet Union in ruins, China rhetorically fending off capitalism even as in reality it adopts a market economy, Cuba wallowing helplessly in the Caribbean, it is not easy to convey to a contemporary audience the American fear of a masterful communism. When Khrushchev in 1956 bellowed out from his United Nations seat, 'We are going to bury you!', shivers went up a lot of spines but not only because Soviet missiles were pointed our way. It was also on account of something that only ever incidentally referred to external threats – our American triumphalism. This tendency, almost as old as the country, was always a bit too triumphal for the facts: our cyclical depressions, our corrosive racism, our mystification toward so many foreign things. To put it bluntly, there has always been for a great many people a lurking fear of falling in this country, of the bottom suddenly and reasonlessly dropping out. Perhaps it is that the causes of our recurring crises were never really understood, but merely passed in the fullness of time. After all, in the late forties there were millions of Americans still alive – myself among them – who had experienced the complete collapse of our banking system, the near-total destruction of our vaunted Navy at Pearl Harbor and the continuing persistence of high unemployment despite so many measures to combat it. Boastful though politicians might be, in the fifties, as always, most people were a lot less naive than really to believe in America's social invulnerability. And now, worse yet, a new militant certainty was suddenly in the air, and one which seemed to have no self-doubts worth mentioning. The quickness with which Soviet-style regimes had taken over eastern Europe and then China was breathtaking for a lot of people, and I believe it stirred up a fear in Americans of our own ineptitudes, our mystifying inability, despite our fantastic military victories, to control the world whose liberties we had so recently won back from the Axis powers.

So, the fears on which the anti-communist crusade was raised transcended the immediate political situation. They also went deeper than politics, right down into sex. Again, it is wise to remember that the Right was not only afraid of communism but also and even more so, if on a different level, of homosexuality. This, oddly enough, became real to me on a certain day in 1977 when I arrived at the Franco-Belgian border crossing without my passport.

The Belgian National Theatre, in 1952, had been the first European theatre to put on *The Crucible*, an exciting prospect in those times when it was still quite uncommon for American plays to be done in Europe at all. The theatre, along with the Belgo-American Association, a business group, invited me to attend the première. In the company of Montgomery Clift, whom I was at the time trying to help through a misconceived off-Broadway production of *The Seagull*, I took the subway downtown to renew my outdated passport. I had read, of course, of people being denied passports by the State Departmemt, but by 1952 it had still not dawned on me that I might be one of them, and so I chatted away with Monte about *The Seagull* as I waited to be called up to the clerk. I showed him the telegram from the Belgo-American Association, and requested the renewal within the week so that I could get to Brussels for the première on Saturday evening, five days hence.

Three days passed with nothing from the State Department. I had my lawyer call the Passport Division. He was soon informed that I was not going to Brussels at all. It had been decided that my presence abroad was not in the best interests of the United States, nothing more, nothing less, and no passport was to be issued to me. And I had even begun to brush up on my high-school French!

I soon learned that in Brussels a faintly farcical situation had developed – and I should say that farce was always a step away from many of the tragedies of the period. Since the play was the first and practically the only artistic evidence Europe had seen of resistance to what was considered a fascistic McCarthyism, the applause at the final curtain was intense and insistent, and since the newspapers had announced that I had accepted the invitation to be present, there were calls for the author. These went on and on until the American ambassador felt compelled to stand and take a bow. A species of insanity was spreading everywhere. Here was the ambassador, an officer of the State Department, acknowledging applause for someone deemed by that department too dangerous to be present. It must surely have struck some of the audience as strange, however, that an author would be wearing a wide diplomatic sash diagonally across his chest, and next morning's papers had loads of fun with the scene, which, of course, could hardly have advanced the best interests of the United States. And naturally those inclined to do so saw this shot at me as one more proof that America was launched on the road to fascism.

Twenty-five years passed like an afternoon, and my wife, Inge Morath, and I were in Paris when the invitation came to attend the twenty-fifth anniversary of that first production of *The Crucible* in Belgium. We soon found ourselves nearing the France–Belgium border on our way to the celebratory production at the Belgian National Theatre. The Douane is passing down the aisle inspecting passports. My European-born wife takes hers out of her bag, and I now realize that it never occurred to me, being an American, to bring a passport since, after all, the Belgians and the French are as close as Jersey and Manhattan and both speak French! Luckily, the Douane officer was a theatre buff and recognized me and let us through, but warned that with the recent outbreak of terrorism in Germany especially, controls had been stiffened at all borders and I would absolutely have to have a passport to get back into France.

As I noted in my autobiography, *Timebends*, the American Consul General, Rossiter, attended the theatre's reception for me that afternoon, and in passing offered to be of help, should I need any, during our short stay in Brussels. Leaping at this I asked if I could perhaps get a duplicate passport, and explained what had happened. Twenty-four hours was a drastically short time to expect a passport to be issued but we had to leave for Germany the next day. Rossiter, unflustered, said he could arrange it if I supplied the usual photos. I couldn't help contrasting this behaviour with what I had experienced twenty years earlier from the State Department, but kept the thought to myself.

Next day, photos in hand, I walked into the consulate. Half a dozen or more employees looked up from their desks and applauded! Rossiter's office door opened and he appeared, noting, I was sure, the flummoxed if pleased look on my face. I heartily thanked him and he said, 'Come inside, if you have a minute. I'll explain why you got it so fast.'

In the fifties, he said, he had spent some six years trying to get his Foreign Service job back after being fired for some unexplained breach which, he was told, marked him as a security risk. With the State Department refusing any further explanation, and the inevitable inference of communist sympathies threatening his future in or out of government, he borrowed money and mortgaged his house to mount a lawsuit against the Department, demanding an exposition of this obscure charge.

At long last he was granted a hearing before his accusers and as judge, our final ambassador to South Vietnam, Graham Martin. No friend of the Left, he was last seen helping to load pro-American Vietnamese onto escaping helicopters the day Saigon fell. Scott McCleod, the ultimate sniffer-outer of security risks, proceeded to tell his story. Rossiter had for a couple of years shared an apartment in Cairo with a known homosexual, period. His continued employment by the State Department could not be tolerated.

Rossiter's turn came. Arriving in Cairo, young and unmarried, on his first post as a fledgling diplomat, he was given a list of available apartments, one of which he picked. Not knowing Cairo, his choice was blind. Thus, he lived a couple of years with his fellow officer who, on strict guard against revealing sexual proclivities that would certainly mean the end of his career, had been careful enough to keep Rossiter from suspecting them. Indeed, this hearing was the first time Rossiter had heard that his co-tenant was homosexual. Ambassador Martin now turned to McCleod and asked if he had anything more; McCleod thought not. The ambassador restored Rossiter to his position, ordered his lost salary repaid to him with interest, and that was that.

'So when you asked me to help with your passport,' Rossiter told me, 'I remembered your problems with the Department, and thought I'd speed things up.' Sometimes things work out, if you live long enough.

What this story says about the level of anxiety about security is obvious, but some of the elements aren't. In succeeding years real traitors would indeed be exposed; in the eighties, one of them sold the Navy's entire secret communications codes, another sold the names of all the CIA's collaborators in the world, and so on. But I recall no mention in these real cases of the culprits being left-wingers or homosexuals. They were all good old boys, apparently, and if one, like Aldrich Ames, who sold the Navy codes, sported high-end Jaguars and Mercedes and was a known alcoholic living far beyond his salary, these were indulgences that any successful American would be inclined to allow himself in pursuit of the good life. What is important to remember is that the sale of one's country, in these cases to Russia, never caused the eruption of any generalized fears in the press or public. One need not look far for the reason; these men had no ideology beyond the money-lust. Which leads inexorably to the conclusion that more than actual subversives were the target of the red-hunt; rather it was the *idea* they represented that was so frightening. We were indeed in an ideological war.

I should explain what I mean by the cynicism and corruption of the red-hunt. By 1956, when the House Un-American Activities Committee subpoenaed me, the tide was going out for the committee, which was finding it more and more difficult to make front pages. However, the news of my forthcoming marriage to Marilyn Monroe was too tempting to be passed by. That our marriage had some connections with my being subpoenaed was confirmed when Chairman Walters of the HUAC sent word to Joseph Rauh, my lawyer, that he would be inclined to cancel my hearing altogether if Miss Monroe would consent to have a picture taken with him. The offer having been declined, the good chairman, as my hearing came to an end, proceeded to entreat me to write less tragically about our country. This lecture cost me some $40,000 in lawyer's fees, a year's suspended sentence for Contempt of Congress, and a $500 fine. Not to mention about a year of inanition in my creative life.

But back to the late forties and early fifties; my fictional view of the period, my sense of its unreality was, like any impotence, a psychologically painful experience. A very similar paralysis at a certain point descended on Salem. In both places, to keep social unity intact, the authority of leaders had to be hardened and words of skepticism toward them constricted.

A new cautionary diction, an uncustomary prudence was swiftly inflecting our way of talking to one another. In a country that a bit more than a quarter of a century earlier had given three million votes to Eugene Debs, a socialist presidential candidate, the very word socialism was all but taboo. Words had gotten fearsome. As I would learn directly from students and faculty in Ann Arbor on a 1953 reporting visit for *Holiday Magazine*, students were actually avoiding renting rooms in the houses run by the Housing Co-operative for fear of being labelled communist, so darkly suggestive was the word 'Co-operative'. On hearing this even I was amazed. For one thing, the 'Housing Co-operative' had had a rather noble ring in the despairing thirties; a number of home-owners, unable to make tax or mortgage payments had had to abandon their buildings, and they had been boarded up. Along came some students who had simply gone in and squatted, taking down the boards, cleaning the places up, fixing roofs, painting walls, and charging next to nothing for rooms. It had been a refreshing moment of action in a paralysed hour, and now the very name they had given it was dangerous to utter. But there was more.

The faculty head of orientation at the university told me, in a rather cool, uninvolved manner, that the FBI was enlisting professors to report on students voicing left-wing opinions, and – some more comedy – they had also engaged students to report on professors with the same views. When I published these facts in *Holiday*, the Pontiac division of General Motors threatened to withdraw all advertising from the magazine if I ever appeared in it again; Ted Patrick, its editor, promptly badgered me for another piece, but I didn't know the reason why for some years.

It was a time – as I would only learn decades later from my FBI record obtained under the Freedom of Information Act – when the FBI had shadowed a guest of mine from a dinner party in my Brooklyn Heights house. The guest's name was blacked out and I have been puzzling ever since about his possible identity. The point is that reading my FBI record in the seventies I was not really surprised to learn this. In the fifties everybody over forty believed their phone was being tapped by the FBI, and they were probably right. What is important here is that none of this was secret; most everybody had a good idea of what was happening, but, like me, felt helpless to reverse it. And to this moment I don't think I can adequately communicate the sheer density of the atmosphere of the time, for the outrageous had so suddenly become the accepted norm.

In the early fifties, for example, along with Elia Kazan, who had directed *All My Sons* and *Death of a Salesman*, I submitted a film script to Harry Cohn, head of Columbia Pictures. It described the murderous corruption in the gangster-ridden Brooklyn longshoreman's union, whose leadership a group of rebel workers was trying to overthrow. Cohn read the script and called us to Hollywood, where he simply and casually informed us that he had first had the script vetted by the FBI, and that they had seen nothing subversive in it. On the other hand, however, the head of the AFL motion picture unions in Hollywood, Roy Brewer, had condemned it outright as totally untrue communist propaganda, since, quite simply, there were no gangsters on the Brooklyn waterfront. Cohn, no stranger to the ways of gangsterism, having survived an upbringing in the tough, famously crime-ridden 'Five Points' area of Manhattan, opined that Brewer, quite naturally, was only trying to protect fellow AFL union leader, Joe Ryan, head of the Brooklyn longshoremen. Brewer also threatened to call a strike of projectionists in any theatre daring to show the film, no idle threat since he controlled their union. Ryan, incidentally, would shortly go to Sing Sing prison for gangsterism. But that was not yet.

Meanwhile, Cohn offered his solution to our problem with Brewer: he would produce the film if I would agree to make one simple change – the gangsters in the union were to be changed to communists. This would not be easy; for one thing, I knew all the communists on the waterfront and there was a total of two of them. (Both of whom, incidentally, in the following decade became million-aire businessmen.) And so I had to withdraw the script, which prompted an indignant telegram from Cohn: 'As soon as we try to make the script pro-American you pull out.' One understood not only the threat in those words but also the cynicism: he certainly knew it was the Mafia that controlled waterfront labour. Nevertheless, had I been a movie writer in Hollywood my career would have ended with that refusal to perform this patriotic idiocy. I have to say that there were days when I wondered if we would end up with an unacknowledged, perhaps even comfortable American fascism.

But the theatre had no such complications, no blacklist – not yet anyway – and I longed to respond to this climate of fear if only to protect my sanity. But where to find a transcendent concept? As I saw it, the difficulty was that we had grown so detached from any hard reality I knew about. It had become a world of signals, gestures, loaded symbolic words, and of rites and rituals. After all, the accusations of Communist Party membership aimed at film writers, actors and directors never mentioned treasonous acts of any sort; what was in their brains was the question, and this created a kind of gestural phantom-land. I did not think of it this way at the time but looking back, as I have said, I think we had entered an ideological war, and in such wars it is ideas and not necessarily actions that arouse anger and fear. And this was the heart of the darkness – that the belief had flourished rather quickly that a massive, profoundly organized conspiracy was in place and carried forward mainly by a concealed phalanx of intellectuals, including labour activists, teachers, professionals of all sorts, sworn to undermine the American government. And it was precisely the invisibility of ideas that was helping to frighten so many people. How could a play deal with this mirage world?

There was a fundamental absurdity in the Salem witch-hunt, of course, since witches don't exist, but this only helped relate it more to what we were going through. I can't recall the date anymore, but to one of the Un-American Committee hearings several Hollywood writers brought piles of their film scripts for the committee to parse for any sign of Marxist propaganda. Of course there would hardly be any-thing that provocative in a Hollywood movie of the time but in any case the committee refused to read the scripts, which I imagined was a further humilia-tion for the writers. But what a cruel irony that these terribly serious Party members or sympathizers, in an attempt to prove themselves patriotic Americans, should feel compelled to demonstrate that their work was totally innocuous!

Paranoia breeds paranoia, of course, but below

paranoia there lies a bristling, unwelcome truth, a truth so repugnant as to produce fantasies of persecution in order to conceal its existence. For example, the unwelcome truth denied by the Right was that the Hollywood writers accused of subversion were not a menace to the country, or even bearers of meaningful change. They wrote not propaganda but entertainment, some of it of a mildly liberal cast to be sure, but most of it mindless, or when it was political, as with Preston Sturges or Frank Capra, entirely and exuberantly un-Marxist. In any real assessment, the worst they could do was contribute some money to Party coffers. But most Hollywood writers were only occasionally employed, and one doubted their contributions could have made any difference to a party so completely disregarded by the American public and so thoroughly impregnated by the FBI into the bargain. Yet, they had to be portrayed as an imminent danger to the Republic.

As for the Left, its unacknowledged truth was more important for me. If nobody was being shot in our ideological war but merely vivisected by a headline or two, it struck me as odd – if understandable – that the accused were mostly unable to cry out passionately their faith in the ideals of socialism. There were attacks on the committees' right to demand that a citizen reveal his political beliefs, yes; but on the idealistic canon of their own convictions, the defendants were largely mute. It was a silence, incidentally, which in the public mind probably tended to confirm the committees' characterization of them as conspirators wrapping themselves in darkness. In the artists' defence, the committees instantly shut down as irrelevant any attempts to explicate their ideas, any idealistic displays. But even outside, in public statements beyond the hearings, the accused relied almost wholly on legalistic defences rather than the articles of the faith in which they unquestionably believed. The rare exception, like Paul Robeson's forthright declaration of faith in socialism as a cure for racism, was a rocket that momentarily lit up the sky. But even this, it must be said, was dimmed by his adamant refusal to recognize, at least publicly, what he knew to be the murders of two Soviet Jewish artists, his good friends, under Stalin's anti-Semitic decrees. It was one of the cruel twists of the time that while he would not, in Washington, display his outrage at the murders of his friends, he could, in Moscow, choose to sing a song in Yiddish which the whole public knew was his protest against Soviet anti-Semitism.

In short, the disciplined avoidances of the Left betrayed a guilt which the Right had found a way to exploit. A similar guilt seems to reside in all sorts of American dissidents, from Jehovah's Witnesses to homosexuals, no doubt because there is indeed an unacknowledged contempt in them toward the cherished norms of the majority. It may be that guilt, perhaps, helps account to some important degree for the absence in our theatre of plays that in any meaningful way confronted the deepening hysteria, which after all was the main event in our culture.

Here was a significant part of a whole generation forced to the wall and hardly a word about it written for the stage. But it may simply have been the difficulty of finding a dramatic locution, a working symbolization that might illuminate the complex fog of the unspoken in which we were living – the smoke signals from all sides were hardly declarations of what they really stood for.

To put it bluntly, the pockets of both sides were stuffed with hidden agendas. On the Right there was, quite simply, their zeal to bring down finally in disgrace the last vestiges of New Deal attitudes, particularly those dreadful tendencies in Americans to set limits around the more flagrant excesses of unbridled capitalism and when in distress to look to government for help. Instead, the Right's advertised goal was the defence of liberty against communism, which, in translation, meant that the poor had no one to blame but themselves.

What the Left were not saying was that they were in truth dedicated to replacing capitalism with a society based on Marxist principles, and this could well mean the suppression of non-Marxists for the good of mankind. Instead, they were simply espousing constitutional protections against self-incrimination. Thus, the fresh wind of a debate of any real substance was not blowing through these hearings, or these terrible years. And so the result was miasma, and on the Left, the guilt of the wholly or partially insincere. The Right, of course, with its professional innocence as the warden of hallowed old virtues in whose defence it is convinced it is forever being persecuted, is always a stranger to guilt, sure as ever that it represents the genuine, if incoherent and stifled, wishes of the majority.

How to express all this, and much more, on a stage? I began to despair of my own paralysis. I was a fisherman without a hook, a seaman without a sail.

On a lucky afternoon I happened upon a book, *The Devil in Massachussetts*, by Marion Starkey, a narrative of the Salem witch-hunt of 1692. I knew this story from my college reading more than a decade earlier, but now in this changed and darkened America it turned a completely new aspect toward me, namely the poetry of the hunt. Poetry may seem an odd word for a witch-hunt but I saw now that there was something of the marvellous in the spectacle of a whole village, if not an entire province, whose imagination was literally captured by a vision of something that wasn't there.

In time to come the very notion of equating the red-hunt with the witch-hunt would be condemned by some as a deception. There were certainly communists and there never were witches. But the deeper I moved into the 1690s the further away-drifted the America of the 1950s, and rather than the appeal of analogy I found something somewhat different to draw my curiosity and excitement.

First of all, anyone standing up in the Salem of 1692 who denied that witches existed would have faced immediate arrest, the hardest interrogation and quite possibly the rope. Every authority from the

Church in New England, the kings of England and Europe, to legal scholars like Lord Coke not only confirmed their existence but never questioned the necessity of executing them when discovered. And of course there was the authority of the Bible itself and the words of Saul which had commanded, 'Thou shalt not suffer a witch to live.' To deny witches was to deny the existence of the Devil's age-old war against God, and this in effect left God without an opposite, and stripped him of his first purpose – which was to protect the Christian religion and good order in the world. Without Evil what need was there for Good? Without the Devil's ceaseless plotting who needed God? The existence of witches actually went to prove the existence of God's war with Evil.

Indeed, it became obvious that to dismiss witchcraft was to forego any understanding of how it came to pass that tens of thousands had been murdered as witches in Europe, from Scandinavia across to England, down through France and Spain. Likewise, to dismiss any relation between that episode and the hunt for subversives was to shut down an insight into not only the remarkably similar emotions but also the numerous identical practices, of both officials and victims.

Of course there were witches, if not to most of us then certainly to everyone in Salem; and of course there were communists, but what was the content of their menace? That to me became the issue. Having been deeply influenced as a student by a Marxist approach to society – if less so as I grew older – and having known any number of Marxists and numerous sympathizers, I could simply not accept that these people were spies or even prepared to do the will of the Soviets in some future crisis. That such people had thought to find some hope of a higher ethic in the Soviet was not simply an American but a worldwide irony of catastrophic moral proportions, for their like could be found all over Europe and Asia. But as the fifties dawned they were stuck with the past they had chosen or been led into. Part of the surreality of the great anti-Left sweep of that decade was that it picked up a lot of people for exposure and disgrace who had already in their hearts turned away from a pro-Soviet past but had no stomach for naming others who had merely shared their illusions. In short, then, the whole business for me remained what Truman had called it initially – not a moral crusade but a political red herring.

Nevertheless, the hunt had captured some significant part of the American imagination and its power demanded respect. And turning to Salem was like looking into a petri dish, a sort of embalmed stasis with its principal moving forces caught in stillness. One had to wonder what the human imagination fed on that could inspire neighbours and old friends suddenly to emerge overnight as hell's own furies secretly bent on the torture and destruction of Christians. More than a political metaphor, more than a moral tale, *The Crucible*, as it developed for me over the period of more than a year, became the awesome evidence of the power of human imagination inflamed, the poetry of suggestion, and finally the tragedy of heroic resistance to a society possessed to the point of ruin.

In the stillness of the Salem courthouse, surrounded by the miasmic swirl of images of the 1950s but with my head in 1692, what the two eras had in common was gradually gaining definition. In both was the menace of concealed plots, but most startling were the similarities in the rituals of defence, the investigative routines. Three hundred years apart, both prosecutions were alleging membership of a secret disloyal group. Should the accused confess, his honesty could only be proved in precisely the same way – by naming former confederates, nothing less. Thus, the informer became the very axle of the plot's existence and the investigation's necessity.

Finally, in both eras, since the enemy was first and foremost an idea, normal evidentiary proof of disloyal actions was either de-emphasised, left in limbo, or not required at all, and indeed finally, actions became completely irrelevant. In the end, the charge itself, suspicion itself, all but became the evidence of disloyalty. Most interestingly, in the absence of provable disloyal actions both societies reached for very similar remedies.

Something called the 'Attorney General's List' was promulgated, a list of communist front organizations, membership in which was declared not so much illegal as good reason to suspect subversive conduct or intentions. If membership in an organization could not be called illegal it could at least be made disgusting enough to lose you your job and reputation. One might wonder whether many spies would be likely to join communist fronts, but liberals very possibly might, and indeed had done so at various turns in the road, frequently making common cause with the Left and with communists during the New Deal period a decade earlier.

The witch-hunt in 1692 had a not dissimilar evidentiary problem, but a far more poetic solution. Most suspected people named by others as members of the Devil's conspiracy, had not been shown to have actually *done* anything – neither poisoning wells, setting barns on fire, sickening cattle, aborting babies or calves, nor somehow undermining the virtue of wives (the Devil having two phenomenally active penises, one above the other, as everybody knew). Rather than acts, these suspect folk need only have had the bad luck to have been 'seen' by witnesses consorting with the Devil. The witnesses might be dismally addled hysterics, but they might also be sober citizens who'd somehow gotten themselves suspected of practising witchcraft and could only clear themselves by confessing and naming co-conspirators. But, as in the fifties, there was a supply of non-hysterical lawyers in and around the witch-hunt, as well as Harvard-educated ministers. And, as accusations piled up, one obvious fact became more and more irritating for them: as they well knew, the normal fulcrum of any criminal prosecution, namely acts, deeds, crimes, and witnesses thereto, was simply missing. As for ordinary people, devout and strictly literal about Biblical injunctions as they might be, they still clung to the old habit of expecting some sort of proof of guilt, in this case of being an accomplice to the Devil.

To the rescue came not an Attorney General's List, but a piece of poetry smacking of both legalistic and religious validity – it was called 'Spectral Evidence'. Spectral Evidence, in normal jurisprudence, had been carefully excluded from the prosecutorial armoury by judges and lawyers, as being manifestly open to fabrication. But now, with society under this hellish attack, the fateful decision was made to allow it in, and the effect was the bursting of a dam. Suddenly, all the prosecution need do was produce a witness who claimed to have seen, not an accused person, but what was called his familiar spirit – his living ghost as it were – in the act of poisoning a pig or throwing a burning brand into a barn full of hay. You could be at home asleep in your bed but your spirit could be crawling through your neighbour's bedroom window to feel up his wife. The owner of that wandering spirit was thereupon obliged to account to the court for his crime. With the entrance of Spectral Evidence the air quickly filled with the malign spirits of those identified by good Christians as confederates of the Beast, and with this, of course, the Devil himself really did dance happily into Salem village and proceeded to take the place apart.

In no time at all people in Salem began *looking* at each other with new eyes, and *hearing* sounds from neighbours' throats that they had never heard before, and *thinking* about each other with new and far deeper insights than their former blind innocence toward one another had allowed them. And now, naturally, so many things that had been hidden or befogged suddenly burst open and made sense. Why, for instance, had London annulled all property deeds, flinging people at each other's throats in fights over boundary lines? Why was the congregation forever turning in on itself in fierce doctrinal confrontations and bitter arguments with ministers who one after another had had to flee the contentiousness of Salemites? Clearly, it was the Devil who had been creeping into people's ears and muddling their brains to set them against each other. But now, now at last, with the Lord's help they had the gift of seeing through darkness, the afflicted children had opened up their eyes to the plot in which unknowingly, like innocent birds in a net, they were all caught. Now, with the admission of Spectral Evidence, they could turn to the traitors among them and run them to their deaths.

I spent some ten days in the Salem courthouse reading the crudely recorded trials of the 1692 outbreak, and it was striking how totally absent was any least sense of irony, let alone humour. I can't recall if it was the provincial governor's nephew or son who with a college friend had come from Boston to watch the strange proceedings. At one point both boys burst out laughing at some absurd testimony: they were promptly jailed, and were saved only by friends galloping down from Boston with a bribe for a guard who let them escape from a very possible hanging.

Irony and humour were not exactly conspicuous in the fifties either. I was in my lawyer's office one afternoon to sign some contract and a lawyer in the next office was asked to come in and notarize my signature. While this man was stamping pages, I continued a discussion with my lawyer about the Broadway theatre, which at one point I said was corrupt, that the art of theatre had been totally displaced by the bottom line, which was all that really mattered anymore. Looking up at me, the notarizing lawyer said, 'That's a communist position, you know.' I started to laugh until I saw the constraint in my lawyer's face, and despite myself I quickly sobered up.

I am glad, of course, that I managed to write *The Crucible* but looking back I have often wished I'd had the temperament to do an absurd comedy, which is what the situation so often deserved. There is something funny in the two sophisticated young Bostonians deciding to trot down to Salem to look in on the uproar among the provincials, and failing to realize that they had entered a new age, a new kind of consciousness. Now, after more than three-quarters of a century of fascination with the great snake of political and social developments, I can see more than a few occasions when a lot of us were confronted by the same sensation of having stepped into another age.

Sometime around 1939-40, with the long Spanish Civil War finished and Franco ensconced, a new European war coming closer, and the decade-long Depression lifting at last, the Hollywood studios began flushing out writers in New York for duty on the West Coast. One recruiter sent by Warner Brothers was named, incredibly enough, Colonel Joy. The Colonel was determined to fill boxcars with writers for shipment west. Most of these 'junior writers' were young and were being tempted with a salary of $250 a week, a pittance by Hollywood standards but munificent from the point of view of the deprived denizens of Union Square, Brooklyn and the Bronx. I was acquainted with four or five writers who were packing their bags, a couple of them contributors to and one editor of *New Masses* magazine, a communist weekly. I was young and naive enough to ask this editor, who also had ambitions as a playwright, why he was going west. 'Don't you realize how many people movies reach?' he replied. But with what were they being reached? I wondered. He then mentioned a recent film with John Garfield, the title of which I no longer recall. 'Didn't you see him standing at that bar and saying, "I fought in Spain"? You realize how many people heard that?' It was an action picture, I recalled, and the line had come out of nowhere and gone nowhere.

'But you know what they'd probably make of that?' I said. 'That he'd had a prizefight in Spain; or a fistfight; or maybe even fought on the Franco side.

About one in five hundred would know he was referring to the Abe Lincoln Brigade and the Loyalist cause.' I was too timid to ask if he would be going west if the salary was $35 a week instead of $250. There is no conflict of principle and interest that we humans cannot find a way to rationalize, as Molière should have taught us three centuries ago, and I mention this incident now only to reaffirm that the so-called militant Left was born to mothers like anybody else.

My disbelief in the crusade, as it was coming to be called, against communism, was in some important part the product of this same skepticism toward the idealism of the crusaders. (Nevertheless, of course, I continued to genuflect toward the shibboleths of the Left, a habit that dies hard.) But I had made a similar misidentification of the new direction of the wind as the fifties dawned, and worse yet, continued making it.

A young film producer whom I didn't know asked me to write a script for a film about what was then called juvenile delinquency. A mystifying, unprecedented outbreak of gang violence had exploded all over New York. The city, in return for a good percentage of profits, had contracted with this producer to open police stations, schools and so on to his camera. I spent the summer of 1955 in Brooklyn streets with two violent gangs and wrote an outline, which, incidentally, was much praised by the priests leading the city's main Catholic youth organization. I was ready to proceed with the script when an attack on me as a disloyal lefty was opened in the *New York World Telegram*. The cry went up that the city must cancel its contract with the producer so long as I was the screenwriter. A hearing was arranged, attended by some twenty-two city commissioners, including the police, fire, welfare and not least the sanitation departments, as well as two judges.

At the long conference table there also sat a lady in sneakers and a sweater who produced a thick folder of petitions and statements I had signed, going back to my college years, provided to her, she said, by the House Un-American Committee. I defended myself; I thought I was making some sense when the lady began literally screaming that I was killing the boys in Korea. She meant me personally, as I could tell from the froth at the corners of her mouth, the fury in her eyes, and her finger pointing straight into my face. The vote was taken and came up one short of continuing the city's collaboration, and the film was killed that afternoon. As we were filing out, the two judges came up and offered their sympathy. I always wondered whether the crucial vote against me came from the sanitation department. But it was not a total loss; the suffocating sensation of helplessness before the spectacle of the impossible coming to pass would soon help in writing *The Crucible*.

As I indicated in my autobiography, the impossible coming to pass was not merely an observation made at a comfortable distance but a blade cutting directly into my life. This was especially the case with Elia Kazan's decision to co-operate with the House Un-

American Activities Committee. Again, the sur-
rounding fears felt even by those with the most
fleeting of contacts with any communist-supported
organization were running high enough to break
through long associations and friendships. Kazan,
after all, had been a member of the Party a mere
matter of months, and even that link had ended years
before. And the Party, moreover, had never been
illegal nor was membership in it. Yet this great
director, left undefended by Twentieth Century Fox
executives, his longtime employers, was told – as he
related to me – that if he refused to name people
whom he had known in the Party years earlier –
actors, directors and writers – he would never be
allowed to direct another picture in Hollywood. This
was before the era of independently financed movies,
and such a threat meant the end of his career in films.

Of course, these names were already known to the
committee through other testifiers and FBI inform-
ants, but exactly as in Salem – or Russia under the
Czar and the Chairman, and in China, Inquisition
Spain, Revolutionary France or any other place of
revolution or counter-revolution – conspiracy was
the name for all opposition. And the reformation of
the accused, quite logically, could only be believed
when he gave up the names of his co-conspirators.
Only this ritual of humiliation, the breaking of his
pride and independence, could finally win the
accused re-admission into the community. Whether
his repentance was wholly or partially sincere, or
wholly or partially cynical, was another question; as

was indeed, whether his accusers had one eye on the next election. But whatever the case the process inevitably did produce in the accused a new set of political, social and even moral convictions more acceptable to the state whose fist, as it were, had been shoved into his face, with his utter ruin promised should he resist.

Seen up close, however, it was all even more complicated; some confessors experienced genuine relief from the secret burden carried by the outsider, and worse yet, from the obligation of continuing support for eroded, half-believed radical credos of their Depression youth. There was even a certain gratitude for having been forced to emerge from the guilt-ridden shadows into the American light, where accepted opinion and openness prevailed, into the blessed country of the majority which never knows guilt.

As described in *Timebends*, I had stopped by Kazan's house in the country in 1952 after he had called me several times to come and talk, an unusual invitation, when he had never been inclined to indulge in talk unless it concerned work. So I had suspected from his dark tone that it must have to do with the UnAmerican Committee, which was rampaging through the Hollywood ranks then. Since I was on my way up to Salem for research on a play that I was still unsure I would write, I called at his house, which was on my route. As he laid out his dilemma and his decision to comply with the committee (which he had already done, as it turned out) it was impossible not to feel his anguish, old friends that we were. But the crunch came when I felt fear, that great teacher, that cruel revealer. For it swept over me all at once that had I been one of his comrades he would have spent my name along with others as part of the guarantee of his reform. Even so, oddly enough, I was not filling up with hatred or contempt for him; his suffering was too palpable for that. It was the whole hateful procedure which had brought him to this, and I believe it made the writing of *The Crucible* all but inevitable. For even if one could grant him sincerity in his new-found crusading anti-communism, the concept of an America where such self-discoveries were mandated, pressed out of people, was outrageous and a frightening contradiction of any concept of personal liberty.

Is all this of some objective importance in our history, this destruction of bonds between people? I think it may be, however personal it may appear. It is a fact, after all, that Kazan's testimony against former associates created a far greater shock than anyone else's. Lee Cobb's similar testimony and Jerome Robbins' co-operation with the committee seemed hardly to matter. And it rudely surprised even people who had had no connection of their own with the Left. It is impossible to be sure about this, but it may be, at bottom, that he had been loved more than any other, that he had attracted far greater affection from writers, actors and others with whom he had worked over the years, and so what was overtly a political act was sensed to have been a betrayal of love. This, perhaps, is what unhinged so many and would continue to do so for the next half century, for since they know, consciously or not, that loyal love is dangerously conditional for them as well, it is alarming to see it proved to be so, no matter what its political justifications.

It is very odd and significant, I think, that in the uproar set off by the awarding earlier this year of an Oscar to Kazan for Life Achievement by the Motion Picture Academy, one heard no mention of the name of any member of the House Un-American Committee. One doubted whether the thought so much as occurred to many people that the studio heads at the time had ignominiously collapsed before the committee's insistence that they institute a blacklist of artists in the movie industry, something they had once insisted was too dishonourable to do and a violation of democratic norms to boot. Half a century had passed since his testimony, but Kazan now bore very nearly the whole onus of the era, quite as though he had manufactured its horrors all by himself, when in fact he was surely its victim, however notable – a characterization which, for opposite reasons, both he and those he had named would vociferously deny.

Since you, or some of you, are historians, I have emphasised history in these remarks, but I doubt if I'd have actually written the play had the question of language not so powerfully drawn me on. The trial record in Salem courthouse, a photocopy of which I was allowed to borrow, had been written by ministers in a primitive shorthand. This condensation gave emphasis to a gnarled, densely packed language which suggested the country accents of a hard people. (A few years on, Laurence Olivier would stage his London production using the gruff Northumberland accent.) In any event, to lose oneself day after day in that record of human delusion was to know a fear not perhaps for one's safety precisely, but of the spectacle of perfectly intelligent people giving themselves over to a rapture of such murderous credulity. It was as though the absence of real evidence was itself a release from the burdens of this world; in love with the invisible they moved behind their priests, closer to that mystical communion which is anarchy and is called God. Evidence, in contrast, is effort; leaping to conclusions is a wonderful pleasure, and for a while there was a highly charged joy in Salem, for now that they could see through everything to the frightful plot that was daily being laid bare in court sessions, their days, formerly so eventless and long, were swallowed up in hourly revelations, news, surprises. *The Crucible*, I think, is less a polemic than it might have been had it not been filled with wonder at the protean imagination of man.

I suppose the pithiness of the language and the directness of its imagery were its main attractions. 'What do you say, are you not a witch?' 'No, I know it not, if I were to die presently.'

'Why, it is false,' an accused responds to a charge,

'I know not of it any more than the child that was born tonight.'

One of my most useful sources was the 1867 two-volume history of the trials by Charles W. Upham, who had been Mayor of Salem, albeit nearly a century and a half after the catastrophe. But there were still some seventeenth-century houses, and a number of descendants of participants in the Delusion, as he called it, whose traditions helped him to see obscure connections in court testimony and to draw detailed maps showing where many of the participants' vanished homes had once stood, as well as lanes and byways, long grown over, where people had once moved cattle and goods. It is rather an amazing book, full of canny insights drawn from obscure contradictions in the testimony and also letters of the era. He was able, for example, to deconstruct a deposition, phonetically written, allegedly by one James Carr, a simple farmer, accusing a Mrs Bradley of witchcraft, and to show that in fact it was written by none other than the perfectly literate Thomas Putnam, the same man who was behind so many false accusations, some of which resulted in the deaths of the accused. More, by mouthing the spelling Putnam used, Upham could guess at the way certain words were pronounced a century and a half earlier. '"Corsely",' he writes, 'no doubt shows how the word was then spoken. "Angury" was, with a large class of words now dissyllables, then a trisyllable. "Tould", "spaking", . . . are spelled just as they were then pronounced".'

From this and other accusatory depositions I was able to begin sounding the language of 1692 Salem on my own tongue, and they ultimately informed my dialogue. I came to believe, incidentally, that they spoke in a kind of brogue with a Scottish flavour. In any case, with the ample history at my elbow it struck me that Shakespeare's string of long plays might be explained by his having the books to dip into whenever he got stuck for more story. Of course it is never quite that easy; any history is so packed with important characters that their merging into compound personalities, along with the condensaton of events, becomes the main order of business. And in the end a new history emerges whose 'truths' may be related to the original facts but do not really replicate them.

The Crucible straddles two very different worlds to make them one, but in the usual sense of the word it is not history but rather a moral, political and psychological construct that floats on the fluid emotions of both eras. As a commercial entertainment the play failed, of course. To start with there was the title: nobody knew what a crucible was. Most of the critics, as sometimes does happen, never caught on to the play's ironical substructure, and the ones who did were nervous about validating a work that was so unkind to the same sanctified procedural principles as underlay the then-current hunt for reds. Some old acquaintances gave me distant nods in the theatre lobby on opening night, and even without air-conditioning the house was noticeably cool. (It reminded me of a remark, allegedly a real one, uttered by a famous Broadway producer of the twenties, Max Gordon, whose play about Napoleon had just flopped. 'I hope I croak before I put on another play where the guy writes with a feather!')

But the problem was also with the temperature of the production. The director, Jed Harris, a great name in the theatre of the twenties, thirties, and into the forties, had decided that the play, which he believed a classic, should be staged like what he called a Dutch painting. In the Dutch paintings of groups everyone is always looking front. We knew this from the picture on the wooden boxes of Dutch Masters cigars. Unfortunately, on a stage such rigidity can only lead an audience to the exits. It would be several years before a gang of young actors, setting up chairs in the ballroom of the McAlpin Hotel, fired up the audience and convinced the critics – and the play at last took off and soon found its place in the world. There were cheering reviews this time, but I couldn't help noting that by then McCarthy was dead. The public fever on whose heatwaves he had spread his wings, had subsided, and more and more people were finding it possible to look into the dying embers and read the terrible message in them.

It is said that no one would buy land in Salem for a hundred years. The very ground was accursed. Salem's people, in the language of the time, had broke charity with one another. But the Devil, as he usually does after such paroxysms, has had the last laugh. Salem refuses to fade into history.

A few years ago the foundations of an old colonial era church in a town near Salem began to sag. The contractor engaged to make repairs dug out some of the loose stones and crawled underneath to inspect matters. There he discovered what looked to him like barely buried human skeletons. Harvard scientists were called in and confirmed that the remains of some twenty-two people were under the church. Now, no one has ever known exactly where the gibbet was located in Salem and the bodies of the twenty-two people hanged there for practising witchcraft have never been found. Moreover, according to one legend they were denied Christian burial as their ultimate punishment.

The scientists wanted to remove the skeletons and try to identify them, but some aged parish leaders, descendants not only of the witchcraft victims but no doubt their persecutors as well, were adamantly opposed. The younger church members were all for it but decided to wait until the elders had passed away rather than start a ruckus about the matter. In short, even after three centuries, the thing, it seems, cannot find its serene, just and uncomplicated end. And oddly enough, something very similar occurred in Salem three hundred years before. After the hunt had blown itself out — after Cotton Mather, having whipped up the hysteria to the point of murder, had finally conceded that supporting the admission of Spectral Evidence had been his dreadful mistake — the legislature awarded, not to all but to some of the victims' families, a few pounds damages along with a mild apology . . . Sorry we hanged your mother, and so forth. But in the true Salem style of solemn bewilderment, this gesture apparently lacked a certain requisite chaos, and so they also included reparations to some informers whose false accusations had gotten people hanged. Victims and victimizers, it was all the same in the end. I suppose it was just the good old American habit of trying to keep everybody happy.

The Crucible is my most-produced play, here and abroad. It seems to be one of the few surviving shards of the so-called McCarthy period. And it is part of the play's history, I think, that to people in so many parts of the world its story seems so like their own. It was in the mid-seventies – dates at my age take on the viscosity of poached eggs – but in any case, I happened to be at my publishers', when another Grove Press author came in. Her eyes filled with tears at our introduction, and she hastened to explain: she was Yuen Cheng, author of *Life and Death in Shanghai*, the story of her six-year solitary confinement under the Cultural Revolution. It seems that on her release, an old friend, a theatre director, took her to see a new production of his in Shanghai of *The Crucible* – she had heard of neither the play nor its author. Listening to it, the interrogations sounded so precisely the same as the ones she and others had been subject to under the Cultural Revolutionaries that she couldn't believe a non-Chinese had written it. And picking up the English text she was amazed, she said, not least by the publication date, which of course was more than a decade before the Cultural

Revolution. A highly educated woman, she had been living with the conviction that such an outrageous perversion of just procedure could only happen in the China of a debauched revolution! I have had similar reactions from Russians, South Africans, Latin Americans and others who have endured dictatorships, so universal is the methodology of terror portrayed in *The Crucible*. In fact, I used to think, half-seriously – and it was not far from the truth – that you could tell when a dictator was about to take power in a Latin American country or when one had just been overthrown, by whether *The Crucible* was suddenly being produced in that country.

The net result of it all I suppose, is that I have come, rather reluctantly, to respect delusion, not least of all my own. There are no passions quite as hot and pleasurable as those of the deluded. Compared to the bliss of delusion, its vivid colours, blazing lights, explosions, whistles and sheer liberating joys, the search for evidence is a deadly bore. In *Timebends*, I have written at some length about my dealings with Soviet cultural controllers when, as International President of Pen, I would attempt to impress its democratic values upon them in their treatment of writers. Moving about there, and in East Germany, Hungary, Czechoslovakia in communist times, it was only by main force that I could dredge up memories of my old idealism which I had attached to what in reality had turned out to be little more than a half-feudal society led by an unelected elite. How could this possibly be? I can only think that a man in a rushing river will grasp at any floating thing passing by.

History, or whatever piece of its debris one happens to connect with, is a great part of the answer. For me it was my particular relation to the collapse of key institutions in the Great Depression, the some-times scary anti-Semitism I kept running into and the Left's thankful condemnation of it; the Spanish Civil War and the all-but-declared pro-fascist sympathies of the British, and Roosevelt's unacknowledged collaboration with their arms blockade of the Repub-lic, the so-called Non-Intervention Policy. Indeed, on Franco's victory, Roosevelt would tell Secretary of the Interior Harold Ickes, according to Ickes' autobiography, that his Spanish policy was 'the worst mistake I ever made'. In a word, out of the great crash of '29 America and the world seemed to awaken to a new sense of social responsibility, something which to the young seemed very much like love. My heart was with the Left if only because the Right hated me enough to want to kill me, as the Germans amply proved. And now, of course, the most blatant and most foul anti-Semitism is in Russia, leaving people like me filled not so much with surprise as a kind of wonder at the incredible amount of hope there once was, and how it disappeared and whether in time it will ever come again, and attached, no doubt, to some new illusion.

So there is hardly a week that passes when I don't ask the unanswerable – what am I now convinced of that will turn out to be ridiculous? And yet one can't forever stand on the shore; at some point, even filled with indecision, skepticism, reservation and doubt, you either jump in or concede that life is forever elsewhere. Which I dare say was one of the major impulses behind the decision to attempt *The Crucible*.

Salem village, that pious, devout settlement at the very edge of white civilization, had displayed – three centuries before the Russo-American rivalry and the issues it raised – what can only be called a kind of built-in pestilence nestled in the human mind, a fatality forever awaiting the right conditions for its always unique, forever unprecedented outbreak of distrust, alarm, suspicion and murder. And for people wherever the play is performed on any of the five continents, there is always a certain amazement that the same terror that had happened to them or that was threatening them, had happened before to others. It is all very strange. On the other hand, the Devil is known to lure people into forgetting precisely what it is vital for them to remember – how else could his endless reappearances always come with such marvellous surprise?

May 1999

Behind *The Price*

Behind *The Price*

The sources of a play are both obvious and mysterious. *The Price* is first of all about a group of people recollected, as it were, in tranquillity. The central figure, the New York cop Victor Franz, and his wife Esther, are not precise portraits of the couple I knew long, long . ago, but close enough; and Gregory Solomon, the old furniture dealer, is as close as I could get to reproducing a dealer's Russian–Yiddish accent which still tickles me whenever I hear it in memory.

First, the bare bones of the play's story: the great crash of 1929 left Victor and his elder brother, Walter, to care for their widowed father, who had been ruined in the stock market collapse and was helpless to cope with life. While Victor, loyal to the father, dropped out of college to earn a living for them both and ended up on the police force, Walter went on to become a wealthy surgeon. The play begins decades later on the attic floor of the decrepit brownstone where the cop and his father had lived, surrounded by piles of furniture from their old apartment which the father had clung to. Now the building, owned by the father's brother, is to be torn down so the furniture must be sold.

The conflict of how to divide the proceeds cuts open the long-buried lives of both men, as well as that of Victor's wife, and reveals the choices each has made and the price that each has paid as a result. Through it all weaves the antic, ninety-year-old furniture dealer, Gregory Solomon, who is yards ahead of them as he tries to shepherd them away from the abyss towards which he knows they are heading.

Behind the play – almost any play – are more or less secret responses to other works of the time, and these may emerge as disguised imitation or as outright rejection of the dominating forms of the hour. *The Price* was written in 1968, and since nobody is going to know it anymore it may as well be admitted that in some part it was a reaction to two big events that had come to overshadow all others in that decade. One was the seemingly permanent and morally agonizing Vietnam War, the other a surge of avant garde plays that to one or another degree fitted the matrices of the absurd styles. I was moved to write a play that might confront and confound both events.

I enjoyed watching an absurd play: my first theatre experiences were with vaudeville in the twenties, after all, and absurdist comics like Bert Williams and Willy Howard, with their delicious proto-shaggy-dog stories and skits were favourites. More, for a while in the thirties our own William Saroyan, who with all his failings was an authentic American inventor of a domestic absurdist attitude, had held the stage. One would not soon forget his *Time* magazine subscription salesman reading – not without passion – the page-long name-list of *Time*'s reporters, editors, sub-editors, fact-checkers, department heads and dozens of lesser employees, to a pair of Ozark hillbillies dressed in their rags, seated on their rotting porch and listening with rapt incomprehension.

The late sixties was a time when a play with recognizable characters and a beginning, middle and end was of course condemned as 'well-made', or ludicrously old-fashioned. (That plays with no characters, beginning or end were not called 'badly made' was inevitable when the explosion of despised rules in all things was a requisite for recognition as modern. That beginnings, middles and ends might not be mere rules but a replication of the rise and fall of human life did not frequently come up.)

Often against my will, however, I found myself enjoying the new abstract theatre and the absurd; for one thing it was moving us closer to a state of dream, and for dreams I had nothing but respect. But as the dying continued in Vietnam with no adequate resistance to it in the country, the theatre, so it seemed to me, risked trivialization by failing to confront the bleeding, at least in a way that could reach most people. In its way, *Hair* had done so by offering a laid-back counter-lifestyle opposed to the aggressive military–corporate one. But one had to feel the absence – not only in theatre but everywhere – of any interest in what had surely given birth to Vietnam, namely its roots in the past.

Indeed, the very idea of an operating continuity between past and present in any human behaviour was *demodé* and itself close to a laughably old-fashioned irrelevancy. My impression, in fact, was that playwrights were either uninterested or incapable of presenting antecedent material altogether. Like the movies, plays seemed to exist entirely in the now; characters had either no past or none that could somehow be directing present actions in any profound way. It was as though the culture had decreed an amnesia as the ultimate mark of the real.

As the corpses piled up it became cruelly impolite if not unpatriotic to suggest the obvious, that we were fighting the past; our rigid anti-communist theology, born of another time two decades earlier, made it a sin to consider Vietnamese reds as nationalists rather than Moscow's and Beijing's yapping dogs. We were fighting in a state of amnesia, quite as though we had not aborted a national election in Vietnam and divided the country into separate halves as it had become clear that Ho Chi Minh would be the overwhelming favourite for the presidency. This was the reality on the ground, but unfortunately it had to be recalled in order to count. And so fifty thousand Americans, not to mention the millions of Vietnamese, paid with their lives to support a myth and a bellicose denial.

As always it was the young who paid. I was fifty-three in 1968, and if the war would cost me nothing materially, it wore away at the confidence that in the end Reason had to return lest all be lost. I was not sure of that anymore. Reason itself had become unaesthetic, something art must at any cost avoid.

The Price grew out of a need to reconfirm the power of the past, the veritable seedbed of current reality, and in that way, if possible, to reaffirm cause and effect in an insane world. It seemed to me that if, through the mists of denial, the bow of the ancient ship of reality could emerge the spectacle might once again hold some beauty for an audience. If the play does not utter the word Vietnam, it speaks to a certain spirit of unearthing the real that seemed to have very nearly gone from our lives.

Which is not to deny that the primary force driving *The Price* was a tangle of memories of people. Still, these things move together, idea feeding characters and they deepening idea. The year in which the play is set, 1968, was already nearly forty years on from the Great Crash, the onset of the transformed America of the Depression decade. It was then that the people in this play had made the choices whose consequences they now had to confront. It had been a time, the thirties, when we learned the fear of doom and had stopped being kids for a while; the time when, as I once noted about the era, the birds came home to roost and the past became present. And that Depression cataclysm, incidentally, seemed to teach that lives indeed had beginnings, middles, and the consequent endings.

Plays leave a wake behind them as they pass into history, with odd objects bobbing about in it. Many of these, as in the case of *The Price*, are strangely funny for such a serious work. I had just finished writing it and with my wife went to the Caribbean for a week's vacation. Hurrying on to the beach in our first hour there we noticed a man standing ankle-deep in the water, dressed in shorts and a wide-brimmed plantation hat who looked a lot like Mel Brooks. In fact he was Mel Brooks. After a few minutes' chat I asked if there was any fishing here. 'Oh God, yes,' he said, 'yesterday there was one came in right there,' and he pointed a yard away in the shallow water. 'Must have been three feet long. He was dead. But he may be over there today,' he added, pointing down the beach.

He wanted to know if I was writing and I said we were casting a new play called *The Price*, and he asked what it was about. 'Well,' I said, 'there are these two brothers . . .'

'Stop, I'm crying!' he yelled, frightening all the Protestants lying on the beach.

Then there was the letter from the Turkish translator who assured me that he had made only one change in the text. At the very end, he wrote, after the two brothers nearly come to blows and part forever, unreconciled and angry, there follows a quiet, rather elegiac moment with the old furniture dealer, the cop and his wife. Just as they are leaving the stage, the translator explained, he had to bring back the elder brother Walter to fall tearfully into the cop's arms. This, because the audience would fear that *the actors themselves* would have had to have a vendetta that could only end in a killing if they parted as unreconciled as the script required. And so, out of the depths, rose the Turkish past . . .

October 1999

Salesman At Fifty

Salesman at Fifty

As far as I know, nobody has figured out time. Not chronological time, of course — that's merely what the calendar tells — but real time, the kind that baffles the human mind when it confronts, as mine does now, the apparent number of months, weeks, and years that have elapsed since 1948, when I sat down to write a play about a salesman. I say 'apparent' because I cannot find a means of absorbing the idea of half a century rolling away beneath my feet. Half a century is a very long time, yet I must already have been grown up way back then, indeed I must have been a few years past thirty, if my calculations are correct, and this fact I find indigestible.

A few words about the theatrical era that *Death of a Salesman* emerged from. The only theatre available to a playwright in the late forties was Broadway, the most ruthlessly commercialized theatre in the world, with the off-Broadway evolution still a decade away.

That theatre had one single audience, not two or three, as is the case today, catering to very different levels of age, culture, education, and intellectual sophistication. Its critics were more than likely to be ex-sports reporters or general journalists rather than scholars or specialists university-trained in criticism. So a play worked or it didn't, made them laugh or cry or left them bored. (It really isn't all that different today except that the reasoning is perhaps more elevated.) That unified audience was the same for musicals, farces, O'Neill's tragedies, or some imported British, French, or Middle European lament. Whatever its limitations, it was an audience that loved theatre, and many of its members thought theatregoing not a luxury but an absolute necessity for a civilized life.

For playwriting, what I believe was important about that unified audience was that a writer with ambitions reaching beyond realistic, made-for-entertainment plays could not expect the support of a coterie of like-minded folk who would overlook his artistic lapses so long as his philosophical agenda tended to justify their own. That unified audience had come in from the rain to be entertained, and even instructed, if need be, provided the instruction was entertaining. But the writer had to keep in mind that his proofs, so to speak, had to be accessible both to the lawyers in the audience and to the plumbers, to the doctors and the housewives, to the college students and the kids at the Saturday matinee. One result of this mix was the ideal, if not the frequent fulfilment, of a kind of play that would be complete rather than fragmentary, an emotional rather than an intellectual experience, a play basically of heart with its ulterior moral gesture integrated with action rather than rhetoric. In fact, it was a Shakespearean ideal, a theatre for anyone with an understanding of English and perhaps some common sense.

Some of the initial readers of the *Death of a Salesman* script were not at all sure that the audience of 1949 was going to follow its manipulations of time, for one thing. Josh Logan, a leading stage and film director of numerous hits, *Mr Roberts* and *South Pacific* among them, had greeted *All My Sons* two years earlier with great warmth, and invested a thousand dollars in *Salesman*, but when he read the script he apologetically withdrew five hundred. No audience, he felt, would follow the story, and no one would ever be sure whether Willy was imagining or really living through one or another scene in the play. Some thirty years later I would hear the same kind of reaction from the theatre people in the Beijing People's Art Theatre, where I had been invited to stage the play, which, in the view of many there, was not a play at all but a poem. It was only when they saw it played that its real dramatic nature came through.

In the 1949 Broadway audience there was more to worry about than their following the story. In one of his letters O'Neill had referred to that theatre as a 'showshop', a crude place where a very uncultivated, materialistic public cut off from its own spirituality gathered for a laugh or a tear. Clifford Odets, with his first successes surely the most hotly acclaimed playwright in Broadway history, would also end in bitter alienation from the whole system of Broadway production. The problem, in a word, was seriousness. There wasn't very much of it in the audience, and it was resented when it threatened to appear on the stage.

So it seemed. But *All My Sons* had all but convinced me that if one totally integrated a play's conceptual life with its emotional one so that there was no perceptible dividing line between the two, such a play could reach such an audience. In short, the play had to move forward not by following a narrow, discreet line, but as a phalanx, all of its elements moving together simultaneously. There was no model I could adapt for this play, no past history for the kind of work I felt it could become. What I had before me was the way the mind – at least my mind – actually worked. One asks a policeman for directions; as one listens, the hairs sticking out of his nose become important, reminding one of a father, brother, son with the same feature, and one's conflicts with him or one's friendship come to mind, and all this over a period of seconds while objectively taking note of how to get to where one wants to go. Initially based, as I explained in *Timebends*, my autobiography, on an uncle of mine, Willy rapidly took over my imagination and became something that had never existed before, a salesman with his feet on the subway stairs and his head in the stars.

His language and that of the Loman family were liberated from any enslavement to 'the way people speak'. There are some people who simply don't speak the way people speak. The Lomans, like their models in life, are not content with who and what they are, but want to be other, wealthier, more cultivated perhaps, closer to power. 'I've been remiss,' Biff says to Linda about his neglect of his father, and there would be many who seized on this usage as proof of the playwright's tin ear or of some inauthenticity in the play. But it is in Biff's mouth precisely because it is indeed an echo, a slightly misunderstood signal from above, from the more serious and cultivated part of society, a signal indicating that he is now to be taken with utmost seriousness, even remorseful of his past neglect. 'Be liked and you will never want' is also not quite from Brooklyn, but Willy needs aphoristic authority at this point, and again, there is an echo of a – for want of a better word – Victorian authority to back him up. These folk are the innocent receivers of what they imagine as a more elegant past, a time 'finer' than theirs. As Jews light-years away from religion or a community that might have fostered Jewish identity, they exist in a spot that probably most Americans feel they inhabit – on the sidewalk side of the glass looking in at a well-lighted place.

As it has turned out, this play seems to have shown that most of the world shares something similar to that condition. Having seen it in five or six countries, and directed it in China and Sweden, neither of whose languages I know, it was both mystifying and gratifying to note that people everywhere react pretty much the same in the same places of the play. When I arrived in China to begin rehearsals the people in the American embassy, with two exceptions, were sure the Chinese were too culturally remote from the play ever to understand it. The American ambassador and the political officer thought otherwise, the first because he had been born and raised in China, and the second, I supposed, because it was his job to understand how Chinese thought about life. And what they were thinking turned out to be more or less what they were thinking in New York or London or Paris, namely that being human – a father, mother, son – is something most of us fail at most of the time, and a little mercy is eminently in order given the societies we live in, which purport to be stable and sound as mountains when in fact they are all trembling in a fast wind blowing mindlessly around the earth.

December 1998